D1568951

So Late to the Party

So Late

to the

Party

Kate Angus

To Robin —

With so much gratitude &
fondness for the Shad & the
best Sister in town! Love, Kate

Negative Capability
PRESS
MOBILE ALABAMA

PRAISE FOR *SO LATE TO THE PARTY*

"Lately I've been reading a Kate Angus poem every morning, so I can start the day falling in love with language. The poems in *So Late to the Party* look at love and lust, loneliness and longing, and treat us to a better understanding of the nuances of humanity. These poems will break your heart."

—Shelly Oria, author of *New York 1, Tel Aviv 0*

"Oh, this book. Don't miss this beautiful book. Kate Angus's debut, *So Late To The Party*, is a deep dive into longing. Perhaps the speaker in 'Is The World A Terrible Place?' gives the best summary: 'Think of lovers.//They will not think of you.' With pitch-perfect rhythm, crackling language, and sly humor ('please do not ever leave me!' is a line from an ode to the American Heritage Dictionary), these poems make us contend with loneliness, heartache, and the devastating passage of time. This collection will grab you by the throat."

—Diana Spechler, author of *Who by Fire* and *Skinny*

ACKNOWLEDGMENTS

My gratitude to the editors of the following journals and anthologies that first published these poems (some in slightly different forms or under different titles):

Barrow Street: "Distant Satellite"

The Best American Poetry website: "Basic Zoology" and "Letter to the Younger Me"

Best New Poets 2014 anthology: "Wild Rabbits Have Sharp Eyes"

Birmingham Poetry Review: "If the Dead Bird in the Gutter Rises Up"

cellpoems: "Later"

Coconut: "This Succession of Bad Weather Days Has Become Demoralizing" and "Sonnet"

Country Dog Review: "Guidance"

failbetter: "Ghost Heart" and "No Wonder"

Gulf Coast: "Last Call"

Indiana Review: "Painters" and "I Have Not Yet Composed a Lullaby for the Fretful Baby in Her Stroller on the Street, But I Did Write a Tiny Love Song for You, American Heritage Dictionary"

Iron Horse Review: "So Late to the Party"

Juked: "In the Award-Winning Movies in My Head, We Are Infinitely Better-Looking and Everything Makes Sense" and "The

Problem Is Not that God Does Not Exist So Much as that He Will Not Bargain with You"

L Magazine: "To the Mustache of the Guy in the "Che Guevara Is My Homeboy" T-Shirt at Odessa's Late the Other Night"

Maggy: "A Little Gothic Tale" and "Intimacy"

Mid-American Review: "If My Life Were a Radio, Lately I Would Prefer Another Station" and "Cosmo Magazine Tells Me I'll Be Alone All My Life"

Poet Lore: "Birth Chart," "In the Morning, I Buy a Dress," "Complicity," "Sublation," "Now Let's Return to Stasis," "Inside My Sleep," "My Life in Retrospect," "Here's a Little Personal History," "Taking Stock of Things," Catechism," "String Theory, "I Do Not Want to Lose Anybody," "In Like a Lion, Out Like a Lamb," and "Is the World a Terrible Place?"

The Saint Ann's Review: "Dear Friend" and "Starter Notes for the Simulacra"

Sub-Lit: "You Keep on Working and I Will Continue Thinking about Wolves"

Subtropics: "Thank You Again, Brooklyn, for the Free Coffee" and "I Will Begin Tagging "Sad Robot, Inc." on Numerous Surfaces Because I Am Sorry I Am Not Always Good at Certain Emotional Intimacies Shared Between Friends"

Third Coast: "Michigan 1986"

The Hairpin: "Fresh Hells"

Tin House online: "In the Museum of What I've Been Thinking"

Satellite Collective's *Telephone: An International Arts Experiment*: "Dioscuri"

"Inside My Sleep" was reprinted in the *Best New Poets 2010* anthology.

"I Will Begin Tagging "Sad Robot, Inc." on Numerous Surfaces Because I Am Sorry I Am Not Always Good at Certain Emotional Intimacies Shared Between Friends" was reprinted on *Verse Daily*

"Painters" was reprinted on Wave Books' Tumbler page

Thank you so much to Sue Walker, Megan Cary, Baily Hammond Robertson, Isabelle Whitman, and everyone at Negative Capability Press. I'm also grateful to Kimberly Steele, Sharmila Cohen, John David West, Matt Cunha and Eric Smith for looking at earlier drafts—thank you for your rigorous aesthetics and for your friendship.

I am very grateful to David Lehman, Meghan O'Rourke, Mark Bibbins and Mike Delp for guidance and friendship in years early and late. Thank you especially to Jack Driscoll and Matthew Zapruder for being the best mentors and pals I could have ever asked for. Thank you also to my students: especially and always Will Simescu, Phoebe Rusch, Wendy Merry, Rachel Mannheimer, and Chase Yurga-Bell.

I am very grateful to Diana Spechler, Marah Strauch, Allison Contey, Elizabeth Bull, Chin-Sun Lee, Shelly Oria, Alison Espach, Barak Smucha, Megan Shutes, Dana Edell, Moira Meltzer-Cohen, Mia Eaton, Alicia Rabins, Freya Rand, Nicolas Amara, Andrew Mastrocinque and Jason Carney. Thanks to everyone at CFER for giving me the community I needed away from my desk. Thanks also to Interlochen Arts Academy at Interlochen Center for the Arts, the Betsy Hotel's Writers' Room, the Mayapple Center for Arts and Humanities, the Wildfjords Trail, and the BAU Institute in Otranto, Italy.

No one
Has lots of them
Lays or friends or anything
That can make a little light in all that darkness.
There is a cigarette you can hold for a minute
In your weak mouth
And then the light goes out,
Rival, honey, friend,
And then you stub it out.

—Jack Spicer, from "For Hal"

TABLE OF CONTENTS

Painters   1

Birth Chart   2

Distant Satellite   3

Thank You Again, Brooklyn, for the Free Coffee   4

To the Mustache of the Guy in the "Che Guevara Is My   5
Homeboy" T-Shirt at Odessa's Late the Other Night

Last Call   7

Letter to the Younger Me   9

In the Morning, I Buy a Dress   10

At Conservatory Water   12

Complicity   13

Hollywood Poem   14

This Succession of Bad Weather Days Has Become   16
Demoralizing

If the Dead Bird in the Gutter Rises Up   17

In the Award-Winning Movies in My Head, We Are   18
Infinitely Better-Looking and Everything Makes Sense

No Wonder   19

Ghost Heart   20

Sonnet   21

I Have Not Yet Composed a Lullaby for the Fretful   22
Baby in Her Stroller on the Street, But I Did Write
a Tiny Love Song for You, American Heritage
Dictionary

Dear Friend   23

I Was Given a Tiny Dragon   24

Intimacy   25

Sublation   26

Now Let's Return to Stasis   27

Inside My Sleep   28

Is the World a Terrible Place?   29

The Problem Is Not that God Does Not Exist So Much   30
as that He Will Not Bargain with You

Guidance   32

My Life in Retrospect   33

Here's a Little Personal History   34

Starter Notes for the Simulacra   35

Click Here   36

Children's Story   37

Dioscuri   39

Parable   40

You Keep on Working and I Will Continue Thinking about Wolves   41

Fresh Hells   42

If My Life Were a Radio, Lately I Would Prefer Another Station   45

Despite the Numerous Things I Might Fixate on, I Am Still Very Lucky to Go to Parties in Brooklyn and Share Cabs with Friends Coming Home   46

Wild Rabbits Have Sharp Eyes   47

Taking Stock of Things   48

Basic Zoology   49

So Late to the Party   50

Catechism   51

I Will Begin Tagging "Sad Robot, Inc." on Numerous Surfaces Because I Am Sorry I Am Not Always Good at Certain Emotional Intimacies Shared Between Friends   53

Later   55

A Little Gothic Tale   56

In the Museum of What I've Been Thinking   57

Cosmo Magazine Tells Me I'll Be Alone All My Life   58

Michigan 1986   60

String Theory   61

I Do Not Want to Lose Anybody   63

In Like a Lion, Out Like a Lamb   64

Notes   67

About the Author   69

This book is for my parents & for Hester—you make everything possible. Thank you.

Painters

In the museum, I was looking at paintings
(blue backdrop, gold minarets)
and remembering the party,
a few days back when Dave said

he used to be a painter. Christine
asked why he stopped and he recited
O'Hara's "Why I Am Not A Painter"
and we laughed. Good

joke. Killing time, smoking
cigarettes; the night full
as a movie set. I will never
want to know the actual reasons. Today,

I turn a corner and I find
seven de Kooning lithographs
for O'Hara. The charcoal swirls
into hats, suits, men

in cities. The poems are mostly
about love; lithographs made
after O'Hara's death. Don't
die, friends. Let's make a pact.

No matter how far
we part or how quickly, it will be
a long time before I stop
thinking of you. When I die (in a blue hotel,

in an ocean, somewhere under
a star-trellised sky), it will take
years to recognize
what I wanted or who I thought

I really was or what I made
disappear before I came here.

Birth Chart

Do you want
to be in love? You can have that.

Lift off the roof
of your skull.

Empty it, leaving
a basin

to collect
rain water.

Birds will flock there
eating insects.

Flurry of feathers
against the dull sky. What else

do you think
would make you happy?

Children. Games.
A red ball thrown

one to another.
Voices calling out

in a field. Horses
stand there. Let them

raise their shy heads
from eating winter clover.

You have a body:
use it.

You have words:
these, on the page.

Distant Satellite

pinwheeling through the dark, could you please alter
your dangerous falling? I think I'd prefer not to be crushed. How minimal

is the difference between movement and sound after hours
with the mail order theremin—listen: wind through a culvert

or water's ghost in the drain or something more
like a whistling. Yes. Like when lips shape the air. I am up all night

as the radiator bangs out its samba. Now my neighbor
downstairs is laughing again. Now a taxi cab sundresses

the street. I don't think right now I feel even the smallest bit lonely.
It's true; certain questions might panic me into pinballing

flashing lights and chimes far away
but eventually I'll be less nervous in speech

and this body. It's just that sometimes your attention
strobes motion sensor lights

like I'm trespassing on one of those cul-de-sacs in the suburbs
where every painted house is fixed like a stamp

to the green envelope of the lawn—
And what I want is to always and silently unseal everything.

Thank you Again, Brooklyn, For The Free Coffee

The morning paper from three days ago
holds in its battered pages
a Cat Power review that says, "Put in
another nickel for that bleary juke box soul." Universe,

accept your gift! Today
my nickel must be compliance
with whatever you care to throw,
despite white feathers beating in my throat

like a tiny blizzard
that chokes the passageways—respiration lately like a winter road
with terrible pile ups.

This is not a drug reference. I am only trying
to breathe as calmly as my yoga teacher means
when she tells us "Be gorgeous postures," although intellectually
I have a problem with that phrase. For the obvious reasons. Listen,

it's amazing how kind people can be, particularly when you have,
in the past and with no ulterior motives, admired pictures of their baby
sleeping (likewise, dogs). Occasionally we can escape commerce like children
chasing leaf scraps in the road. I don't want it

to just be a trade, your smile. On those days
the windows of one's overpriced apartment
twerk in their ill-fitting frames.
Let the building tumble. This will be one way
to learn equanimity: such a flowering
of dust at our feet.

To The Mustache Of The Guy In The "Che Guevara Is My Homeboy" T-Shirt At Odessa's Late The Other Night

Furry worm, red herring, blood-engorged
leech. Anemone waving fronds
to hide the nether regions of the face.
Feathery lost earring on the ground I do not stop

to contemplate because always it seems
I am walking very fast. Borscht's
ghost, remnants of a clown's kiss,
inflamed bivalve's upper lip. Last night,

I closed my eyes and ten thousand
people died while I was sleeping. I wake
up and there are more. I am very lucky.
I drink coffee and read the paper.

I am surrounded by friends who tell me
this is a benevolent universe,
and sometimes I believe them. You,
mustache, hide the secret sorrow

of a man whose perfect mix tape
was stolen from him in his sleep
and who awakens to a forgotten
playlist. Mustache, you know

one should not offer unsolicited
advice: to shave or not to shave,
to leave town or stay, to find new jobs or break up
with lovers, to change our lives in any way,

because this leaves us open
for a deluge in return. It's late
and already I am sleepy thinking of the legion
of my faults: lassitude, inordinate

shyness, the pointless hungers of my noisy
infant heart that keeps on wanting
when I should not want. Mustache, you live
perched above the lip and see all.

You can sense the musculature
turning. You live below the nose
and thus take in the world
with all its promises.

Last Call

Here's to the futile gesture—Dave piggybacking me across the street
under the blown inside-out tulip of my orange umbrella in a rain that sluices down

like discordant strings. And Manhattan in thunderstorms: how lightning sparks less
incandescent than slogans writ in neon that would sell us things. I believe

in the bureaucrats gnawing pencil tips until taken by sleep, dreaming
at plywood desks as they try to outlaw with crumpled paper

far-away guns. The cold coffee styrofoam cradles bitter.
The pool of feeble light. Let us raise a cracked glass

to the woman with a face like a rough wooden sculpture
who, on the bus each morning, smiles. Let us imagine

she's not lonely and the right person will, sometime tomorrow, sit
down and hold her hand. That there's not a finite amount

of love and happiness here, and the world isn't really a cruel restaurant
where some of us are eternally emptying our pockets so lint falls out

like snow but we still can't seem to buy what we need,
while, at the next table, our friends

gorge on chilled oysters and swill rivers of champagne. Why
don't they see us? How could anyone ignore such need,

and go on clinking silverware that flashes
under chandeliers like paparazzi, and still they are smiling

and not finding us grants or lovers who would actually love us
or jobs that fulfill us as human beings? And yet today alone I walked past

at least seven different people
who I might have saved with some perfect combination

of the right words or a kiss or twenty dollars,
who I could have helped at least for a little while.

And did not do so. I have stopped trying
to cause change in this world. If I love

the caped hero who rescues the sad girl from her demons
and thus, by extension, saves us all, sometimes

I want just as much
the digital set of a city burning, the grenades you can throw

at the house in the distance
so the collapsing and chaos happen at the furthest edge

of whatever you once might have touched. And even the plates
stacked neatly behind your white kitchen cabinets,

don't they want a chance
to make their own broken music on the street?

Letter To The Younger Me

Hello, darling. The sky is gray
this morning, like an old wool blanket left
in the rain. In the bookstore,

I misheard someone asking
for "the graphic novel" as them wanting "the death
of the novel" and I thought, "of course." How are you

getting along? Lately, I keep trying
to peel myself like an apple, pare everything down, open up
like envelopes or doors. It isn't working—

so much easier to watch
the march of digital numbers pressing forward
under the smooth surface of the clock. These minutes:

orderly little lemmings plunging
into the sea or they're the small enameled cars
I'd make a caravan of and push

so they tumbled
off the white wicker snow-cliff
of the couch. Oh clanging

against the tiled sunroom floor. Come back,
sun on the floor, slow-moving
trapezoidal shape projected in

through the window when I had
all the hours left
in the world.

In The Morning, I Buy A Dress

Black and shiny as a stapler
or the metal carapace
of some villain's spaceship. It is fit
equally for funerals and parties: a little more
than I can afford. In the afternoon,

it's raining. The umbrellas
turn themselves inside out:
now metal spokes
are a broken armor. Gray streets, skies
like sodden newspapers. I come home

to find two men
snoring in the vestibule. Their breathing
steady, loud as engines. One man's foot half-
blocks the door, and the shorter man
nestles in—they are like

when you crack a walnut shell
and see pale flesh protected
but still vulnerable. Of course, I hurry past
thinking, how do I navigate this? What happens
if I wake them:

will they hurt me, should I feed them?
And then that Rilke poem about a white marble fragment
that tells me I must change my life. It's late at night.
The black dress hangs
in my closet. The neighbors sleep heavily

in the dark upstairs. What good
do these words do? I just make a place
where I cobble incidents together
into a cramped confessional—look at the fretwork patterns
votive candles cast

on the ground, such dark lace inscribed
by the flickering light. The incense is a little bitter.
There's no absolution for inaction. I wake up

to daybreak cold and sunny, an empty vestibule.
Easter Sunday. Young girls with careful ringlets
hold hands with their fathers. Matrons in elaborate hats
are stately barges sailing through the sea.

At Conservatory Water

Surrounded by cedars in Central Park, the basin's a bad penny
copper green. The wind scrapes waves across stagnant water

in serrations like a knife's trail dragged errant over bark. Toy sailboats
drift like husks pulled from heartland corn and discarded,

a flurry like feathers on the chicken-scratched dirt. No—
no farmland and nothing's in ruin here. The hulls gleam,

sails unfurl white as laundry, a circle of red stars emblazoned
near each mast and below every hull, a tiny motor. Radio signals

pulsing through water: direction transmitted by old men. See them
clutching control-sticks on benches, happy in their blankets; small men

keeping warm inside woolen wombs. Who doesn't want to go backward?
Legion, the things I wish to redo. Downtown, where I live, the vampires

are dressing up for the night. Beneath fancy clothes, it's easy
to snicker like a bag full of knives and sometimes I still want

to be so angular I'm the air's sharpest music when I walk. It's possible
money might be all the pointy teeth anyone might ever need. It's like that

when the world is ripe and you're hungry. Some mornings
I break from sleep mouthing "I'm sorry" to the factory I dream

where workers make munitions people three degrees removed
will drop in my name. Is this histrionic? I wake up

with dull brown water sloshing in my chest
like a cistern's brackish dregs. Tell me how do I drain it?

I would like to be clean. Where is the candle I can light
to make the invisible ink show through? What good does it do

to have every secret thing come forth blazing?

Complicity

The piece of left-over pizza in the cardboard box
stares up at me; one sausage an accusatory eye.
The guilt I feel is a little like when one is presented
with a fish, silver in its skin, resting
on a glazed blue plate garnished
with a slice of lemon
sickle-shaped and pale yellow
as the moon. The thing still swimming
in olive oil and herbs. Or it's like when your eye passes over
the trophy head of a shot stag that now looks down
at the family gathered
around the mantelpiece, sipping brandy. Oh poor Falada,
in that fairy tale. Your head
shorn of your body and nailed
above the gate where you watched the tide
of people flowing in and out
of the city. Magic horse
who still spoke and saved the princess
forced to earn her keep as a goose girl—the impostor
who betrayed her mistress to rise above her station
was then dragged through the streets
inside a nail-studded barrel until she died. Where
is the fairness? In the story,
the princess is good
and deserves her mother's blessing which brought speech
to an animal's dead mouth. And surely
the horse did not deserve to die. But that the laws of nature
rearrange themselves the most
for the born wealthy
also cannot be denied. Privilege does not mean
that anyone inherently is better. I write this
and I must remember as I sit here
at my desk in my apartment in a city
whose wars mostly happen very far away.

Hollywood Poem

Good morning, morning
(6 a.m.) with your dark shade
of night's last curtains
about to be swished back

by sunlight's vigorous broom. The black
countdown to dawn dissipates
when neighbors (above, below,
and next to) wake up

to wake up everything
with their televisions and their walking.
Do you have a bone to pick? I do. Clavicle,
the shoulder girdle's little key

that rotates on its axis
where the shoulder is abducted
(a movement that draws a limb away
from the body's median). Not to mention

how that word echoes music (Baroque,
the late Medieval). Clavichord,
today I love you best
because you strike brass or iron strings

with little metal blades called tangents.
Vibrations do the rest. Better even
than Australia's Weather Harp
where wind passing over wires and goatskin

is too much like the soundtrack
to an artsy Western—not much talk,
and the corrupt local sheriff rapes
the brothel keeper. In the last shot

the cowboy's betrayed body
curls fetal in a stream. His brother's
warm gun; his horse run away. Wait;
she noses her soft muzzle down

to nuzzle our hero with whiskery kisses.
Blood dilutes in the rushing water, but see
how I've given you
an almost happy ending.

This Succession Of Bad Weather Days Has Become Demoralizing

All afternoon raining and I have been thinking about money
which is lately a thought inseparable

as hair and my scalp: you'd need razors, well-honed,
and steady hands. In the movies, rain is pennies from heaven

or lemon drops or men. In life, bills. Nobody's singing this.
If my body moving is a table knife through butter

(water-thick air as I walk) or, better, a ship traversing
certain paved seas

(increase speed and my shirttails
and hair billow dark sails), then these damp gray hours

are a wool sweater and the day a terrible mother
who would cover my nose and mouth with it, perhaps as a radical way

to spare me any future bad dreams. I am so tired
and yet I know I am luckier than most. History tells us

it has always been terrible: if you want further knowledge,
read the stories entrails spell on the ground. Profligate,

I'm no better than anyone and, so, overheat canned tomato soup.
Sometimes there's a pattern like how, meeting Marah for coffee, I saw

twin silver star-shaped balloons caught in a sky of green leaves.
And, today, a child's toy whale in the gutter

bobs almost merrily bright blue. Only once in a while I still think
about rearranging the world so I wake up to listen

as you whisper all your childhood
tenderly in the down spiral-staircase of my ear.

If The Dead Bird In The Gutter Rises Up

Tell me that this morning's not collusive
when already I've dropped the coffee pot
—in shards!—and, outside, nearly stumbled
on a pigeon decaying like a heap of autumn

on the ground. Little bird, some people say
you are a rat with feathers but please
flap your wings anyway. Let them be as wet sheets in the wash
furiously folding and unfolding, water droplets flying forth

like a broken tiara's rhinestoned
scattering. Like dreams of bad childhood ballet.
Manhattan should be patched
with pokeweed and chicory

or inlets where unshuckable
oysters grow nacreous
under river-clouding muck. Maybe a hawk
to soar above. But then so much less a city.

Perhaps it's better just to learn
how not to want. I'd like to have
this morning once again
or know how to make my life

a palindrome so there's sense in it
from either direction. That won't happen.
I'd like the bird
to not be dead. It's important

to be permeable. To pay whatever bills
are now past due.
To differentiate between being sad
or only old barn dilapidated.

To imagine a certain kind of waltz
so I can shamble
like there's a circus bear inside me
as I amble solitary down my street.

17

In The Award-Winning Movies In My Head, We Are Infinitely Better Looking And Everything Makes Sense

If it begins with distance, distance is bridged. Let's say a meadow
with deer running close together, their movement the sped-up avalanche

of leaning toward someone I want to kiss. In the movie, I'm sure
that I do. If no one likes this setting, it can be changed to the shuffle

of a deck of steel standing end on end; what we call buildings.
The windows in winter sun glint bitterly in downtown Manhattan

where, each morning, commerce puts on her innocuous clothes.
If I sound furious, I probably am. Aren't we all just a little bit tired

of walking around unlovely, beneath billboards that vulture
the streets? In them everyone is flat and so easy to read. I am sick

of being clandestine. I will put it on the table, see—not like a spread of cards
which could indicate potential cheating, but an unfurling

like a magician's scarf from a hat. I want that flourish: what I mean to say
pulled forth like that. Shouldn't communication be simpler—

just jump-cut childhood and montage the rest? But don't I so often think
that understanding equals reading all the books on someone else's shelves

or that I can braille the fingering of chosen songs
and parlay an echoed movement into seeing what's behind the skull?

And just as often I might say, "World, take my keys.
Here's an address and a time to meet me. Rummage through possessions.

If you are sleepy, use my bed." Let it be enough.
Can't any of us project without talking? Turn off the lights

and unspool film through that tiny hatch, the opening
where a small light and a dark room do the rest.

No Wonder

Spring's for suicides—all those things blossoming: crocuses,
hatched birds, young lovers. Winter

matched my mood at least: bleak, brackish,
dirt-swirl dregs under ice in the cistern.

Now everything is sunlight, warm, an ambergris
evening where the girls are young as I no longer

and walk with tall men in Noah's Ark pairs holding hands.
Look at their breezy little dresses, floral prints.

Look at their long and flowing hair. My old dog
yipes and groans on the cushion by the rib-caged radiator

flecking steam and chips of silver paint. My skin is
a dry wooden floor. Ravens are a gif flapping into the distance

up the left side of my open browser window. Remember
when an open window meant only air?

Ghost Heart

The ghost heart was invented by scientists
whose soap solution

(more brine than froth and foam)
burst all the living cells

in a pig's heart and left behind
only the protein structure.

Decellularized, this heart becomes a trellis
where stem cells like little seeds grow in the dark

and flourish
into a heavy fruit we later harvest.

The scientists have successfully implanted
these hearts tissue-engineered

into rats and pigs. This is a kind of agriculture:
flora, fauna. The ghost heart is white

and luminous, semi-translucent
as a surgeon's glove. It glistens like a snail's

slick mapping or mother-of-pearl. What kind of structure
was I for you? Is there an echo

that resides inside to sometimes remind you
how I was once something nacreous, a temporary

necessity in the bioreactor
encircled by your ribs.

Sonnet

I touch myself; I dream. There are things
I shouldn't tell you, but sometimes I do.
If you live on the other side of the country,
we might as well inhabit pages—characters
who walk through chapters, not people
typing messages to each other in rooms. It's true
one of us might occasionally imagine
a hotel where our bed sheets are a flurry
like enormous swans' wings
and two glasses of cool water form twinned oases
or a pair of clear eyes. The tulips
in the vase on the nightstand are red like little mouths,
closed as matrons' purses,
or rooms we don't go into in our lives.

I Have Not Yet Composed A Lullaby For The Fretful Baby In Her Stroller On The Street But I Did Write A Tiny Love Song For You, American Heritage Dictionary

Dictionary whose spine is cracked,
you are not a jail for words; you are
a little owl. Over the peat moss, over the bog,
you are flying. One billionth

of the letters you contain
slip as flour through my fingers; the rest
I have not even learned yet—please do not ever leave me!
Someday we will drive

through Iowa or somewhere equally flat
with you, shotgun, beside me. Open the window:
let us not be cut off
from that passing landscape

of cows and swelter. Our future is,
like everybody's, at least semi-infinite.
In the occasional arrhythmic night
when I startle out of sleep, dictionary,

you are solid on the table. What does indebtedness
mean? Not just the definition,
my sad heavy friend, but what I owe
you as I infinitely open.

Dear Friend

I was lying on the floor not thinking about much of anything. Grit caught
in the furthest corner of my eye much like children

seeking treasure in caves who are trapped
when the low tide gives way to the large return

of the sea. Poor children; they will drown—swept beneath the waves
with golden trinkets in their hands, and then their bones

are halfway to China. Similarly, my eyes will eventually tear
and so clean themselves through medicinal sorrow. This voice

that asserts itself through me is not always me,
in the same way that the wind makes an eerie sound

like ghosts as it passes over the face of the waters. In French,
le vent means the wind. This is a whistle. Much like God,

who, in a fairy tale, hums or softly sings
as he brushes the tangles and starfish

from his daughter, the ocean's, long hair. Neither my father
nor any lover has once told me a bedtime story

that I can recall. I have been told many things, certainly,
and have, like a sock puppet, been picked up and placed

on the high narrow shelf of certain beds in various locations,
or I have gone there hand in hand as if I or the other

were a docile enough sheep, not knowing if leading or led,
toward a verdant pasture or the abattoir, but anxious

enough to get there, as if it were the going that mattered
because what an unfurling either way: either of your arms

and my legs when into each other we eventually tumble
or the poor dumb animal's slit throat as blood reddens

the sawdust on the floor, or the green field glimpsed
not so far away now through an opening door.

I Was Given A Tiny Dragon

folded from gold foil—origami; gift from a barkeep
like a secret wizard, his beard a dirty river.

Of the two German words I know
wizard is one (*Hexenmeister*); the other signifies

a process carried out in imagination only
(*gedankenexperiment*) rather

than performed in the real world.

Oh, the infinite
number of times

I have closed my eyes
to unbutton your shirt, sliding

each little disc free from its hole
as deliberately as letting

a river swallow

tossed stones. So many things
I would put in a box labeled

what I want to do to you: what it is like to be hungry
and open the door

to a dark room filled entirely with apples.
Through the window, slice

of the cold moon.

Intimacy

Inside the fig
          the wasp
germinates
          new fruit
all those things
          you hate most
are blazing
          white sun
on white rocks
          mirrors
in the summer
          dirty hands
dirty feet
          and your dirty
mouth
          that makes a viper
out of language
          to poison
everything
          it's just a little
nighttime
          conversation
scorpions
          hiding in the fruit basket
scuttle
          along the floor
a momentary
          florescent shimmer
in dark corners
          and you open
those shapely
          horned-moon claws
and let
          your tail unfurl

Sublation

The body is a projection of the mind
existing beyond itself in space. Flesh, and tendons

threading bone, and veins where blood washes like an ocean
through the cells as the mitochondria wave their tiny tentacles

in that tide like a host of cephalopods or like reeds in river muck.
Encasing this, the pelt. Stupid mind, you are always

doing something with this body: the mouth above
that won't shut up, everything below that keeps on wanting

when I should not want. Let's say I'm in a garden
constellated with bottles and cigarette stubs, feral cats

and the slick trails left by slugs. There are friends here, and someone is
someone I should not be thinking of. Dear terrifying body,

you'll send out little missives shaped by your dirty mouth
and they will sink like paper boats. You wanted schooners

that would come back laden with everyone's affection.
You'll use your hands to grasp at things or stop

and flutter hapless in the air
like birds not sure of safe landing. Entirely useless

body, could you please not want? The mind
is telling you to stop. It seems you will keep me up

until daylight cracks its one cold blue eye open
to gaze malevolent at the departing dark.

Now Let's Return To Stasis

What kind of boat is this? Capsized;
what the night's become. Outside
the rain comes down and down.

Strays and rats shiver
inside their trash-heap homes; leaves and debris
in gutters drown. Inside, the dog

beneath the bed scratches long claws
into the floor. I am reading *Dream Songs.* I will sleep
alone. Travelers who have been—

however briefly—inside my body, let your ghosts
go home. I will make them coffee; here are
provisions for the road. I don't want

to be a way-station
but, sooner satiated,
sooner gone. It's time to erase

any patterns we've inscribed.
We'll chant that children's rhyme
where you count backwards

and thus categorically
make untouched each other's
skin. To be trapped

as an isolate memory
in the snapshot collection of your mind
is boring. Burn that album. And, in turn,

if you see the you
in any of these poems as a mirror, break
it and let the shards slice your hands.

Inside My Sleep

You wrote three poems
to explain your absence. Someone else
was a broken red cup

on the floor. This collection of words
arrived this morning as if a train
inside me had carried them from a deep forest

to a city closer to the surface layers
where the outside world
always tugs on my skin. Other words

have less direction but are a feeling
more like a concrete thing. Absence
is also a razor—pliable blade in the mouth. Nesting

is a curled fetal motion, the tiny "g"
the umbilical cord hanging down. If a word is a sound
then "asp" is a hissing

slither around the corner
in the dark. "Hasp" is not just a door lock
but air's rattle in an old man's mouth—

this is a little like dying
and so are the stagnant ponds that fester within. Bogs
where the water has no current. Algae blooms

a wild bilious green. Dragonflies skim
over the surface, shimmer
eye-blue as bluebottle flies do when,

trapped on the wrong side of the window,
they hurl themselves over
and over again against glass.

Is The World A Terrible Place?

The world is a terrible place.
Look at the sea.
All those little waves swallowed by others.

And, beneath the surface, the tiny fish that flicker
like colored ribbons?

Swallowed by larger fish
and by seals. Seals by sharks. Sharks and orcas fighting

until the ocean around them froths bloody
as the sea birds wheel and shriek overhead.

It is like this with people also.
Your father went into your mother
and so you were made.
You rested inside her
in a long hibernation, a tiny vampire bat
curled upside down
in a cave, feet clinging to the ceiling.
Then you tore her apart.

Think of lovers.

They will not think of you
but they may wake up in the dark
and mutter something to themselves using your inflections
or brush the hair
away from their eyes as if with your hand.

And then there is God
who is always giving us the bread of his body
and his sour wine blood, saying, "Eat this. Drink this."
when, all the while, it is his earth

full of mouths that wait to swallow us.
It is enough to make me sick.
The world is full of such terror and still we cannot stay.

The Problem Is Not That God Does Not Exist So Much As That He Will Not Bargain With You

I have a tree growing entirely
inside me: roots anchored
in the pelvic basin, and its top sprawls out leaves
and tender branches from my skull.
It is a Black Maple. In cold and dark,
we turn sap into sugar. Consequently, these days,

I am thinking about death: mine and others. Death
on the Nile.

Murder on the Orient Express.

Death in the Afternoon.
There were times, years ago,

I was very close
to stepping out in traffic's current
as the great white shark
of a city bus (in size, equivalent,
but you must substitute velocity
for teeth) bore down. Sometimes,

I would lull myself imagining
a pistol in my mouth. To fall asleep
thinking this was comforting. Insert
whatever image you prefer here: cigarette,
pacifier, bottle, cock. I was that tired.
I missed Tom that much. Last night

the bar was brown-paper-bagful packed
with friends like Concord grapes held together

by the supple vine

of Alicia singing about how God turned Miriam white with leprosy.
Because she questioned, her skin peeled off and fell like loose pages

from a broken-binding book. I don't know
what's made me so entirely happy these past few years, buoyant

as an empty Pepsi bottle tossed in the Cuyahoga and through the muck
still bobbing unflappably my way along. World,
I want to ask: how did I manage to find you?
And thank you for letting me come back.

Guidance

In the old stories there are dark woods
where you must find your fortune, somewhere inside a wolf

or in a house that stands on restless chicken legs in a clearing.
The path's illuminated: lanterns made from skulls.

One witch rides a mortar and pestle; another will let you lick
sugared walls to grow fat. Occasionally luck sparkles

and you come home with a prince, with a handful
of magic beans, or that mixed blessing of literal eloquence

when each word in your mouth is a diamond. On the one hand,
inordinate riches; on the other, you can never again whisper

and must always stay silent in bed or else you and your lover
will be sleeping on stones. Bright shiny ones. I am not very good

at taking the long view. When young we are told
we can be so many things. Here's a snapshot of me today:

a sleeping machine, a bitter little robot, an old car
where you must turn the key over until rusty gears shift.

I am all dead leaves! In a pile where the wind and the children come.
It will not be so easy to leave this world after all;

there are cupcakes and, on Molly's kitchen table, plastic ducks in a row
on a mirror that mimics a pond: her daughter's first grade diorama.

Small pebbles and reeds and soon, from a bottle, she'll add what's called
Realistic Water. Dear ships in a bottle, tiny trees

unshedding always, it seems that it's true: you can
buy a small anything. Campfire, tombstones,

pile of snow-dusted logs. Not so in the larger world, which is fine.
We're not supposed to want very much after all.

My Life In Retrospect

There was so much
I did not understand: it was like climbing
ten mountains and, on top
of the mountains, swarms of little birds
eating from the trees. The fruit

plucked from verdant leaves
with cold beaks; pits
scattered below
like bloody stones.
It was a good life. Full

of dinner tables. Friends and family
across the glittering candle sticks. Dog
on the floor grinning up
for scraps. Once in a while,
from another room—closed off

and far away—a baby wailed.
The door was locked. Inside,
my husband rocked the baby
in his arms. Calming, like a rowboat anchored
in a river. Perhaps

there was another baby—maybe three
or four; the nursery walls
lined with books and travel posters. "Look
at that castle," my husband
tells the children. "Someday we'll play catch

beside the Loire." The babies coo and gurgle
and look up at him
as they roll their big round eyes.
I am passing goblets of wine
around the table: slosh, spill.

My husband sings quietly
in the nearing dark.

Here's A Little Personal History

Tom's the monster in the box;
Rochester's wife locked
up in the attic. What do you call
lithium's language? I say,

chalk revelations scrawled on the board,
but as half-erased equations. Is death the same
as bipolar? No. There's no sitting shiva
and no wakes, although excessive drinking,

and the tendency to avoid showering
for pleasure or to begin draping mirrors
in black sheets may arrive. But someone might
contort himself cross-legged

hours at a time to study Augustine
or Torah; chant Sanskrit mantras;
hit a gong (purloined); try yoga; imbibe
his piss as Eucharist wine; explain everything's

a radio signal; read all text as directions.
Drive. Think of it this way: the mind's
as much machine as anything. Here's a car
whose imbalance veers the driver

against concrete embankments. Things collide.
That doesn't work. Brain's not always so easily
recalibrated; body's not a chassis
inside which we ride. What is the length

of obligation? How many words are coins
swallowed by the pay phone
if I don't answer? Please stop talking.
Here's a shoebox full of twigs and dry grasses

where the insects hide. Here is the mind
as a storehouse for stringed instruments
untuned. Here's a broken window;
now the wind comes through.

Starter Notes For The Simulacra

A long time ago, I had no name. Under an immensity
of cracked white paint branching out the way glass shatters,

I was a doughy blob. Later, as I grew, I found there is a world
of molded plastic people at our feet. They climb

twine ropes suspended from the kitchen cabinets
or, depending on the child, are carried

to church or school or synagogue
in the dank cloth rooms that are dark pockets.

Whatever happened next I don't remember. The teenage years
were sharp and squirmy. Things then learned and mostly now forgotten

include native trees and bird songs, star map navigation skills (now lost),
Civil War troop movements, and certain interactions

that pertain to furtive hands and mouths. Additional items
owned and entered into inventory consist of a host of insecurities

best compared to bats: all these feelings
hibernate by day, soar and swoop once the world is dark,

and, because of their innate use of homing system radar,
cannot be displaced. Following adolescence, additional instruction

in lecture halls and under fluorescent office lights.
Somewhere I still have notes. In the coat closet you'll discover

boxed up photo albums and various testimonials scrawled
on letters postmarked years ago. I think you'll find my life

welcoming enough. The spare key's on the kitchen table.
And the dog's been fed. The lover prefers his coffee black,

although I think you know this; tell me when our doubleness began.
Already I am leaving. Whatever haunting happens here, you will do for me.

Click Here

to be directed to your new beekeeper, promises
the ad on Google Chrome. No, I'm misreading: on second glance,

it promises a new bookkeeper instead of apoidea, a classification
I learned just now. How would I live

without the diligent kobolds of Wikipedia
scurrying to collect knowledge—gold nuggets hacked out

in long nights of tireless research. They use brain-axes; they trundle
information from the dark mines of JSTOR and Wordpress

to the surface where it shines on my computer screen
white light like mystic video game castles

as I sit here typing to you. I should give them bowls of cool milk;
loaves of bread warm and soft as my hands

which do no hard labor and grow little callous shields
only when I lift weights and swing from metal pull-up bars

in an attempt to be prettier. I do my best,
but most days are still a waterfall

of failures. Stacks of frozen cookies gobbled like Ms. Pac-Man ghosts.
The absent crush whose clipped words are polished pieces of brass

I carry in my pockets into dreams. We live in a world
where adding the x that once meant extinction and an o

that gapes open as a hole you could fall through
is enough to salvage the sign off of an email as romantic; it's so easy to see

what you want to. Fata Morgana (fairy castles in the air); oases
as you crawl desert sands. Flirtation. Despair

as each morning you cobble together comfort in cups of coffee
lined up to bridge the long afternoon like lily pads you leap across

to get through this life you know damn well
you're living and never intended to.

Children's Story

For a while, the wolf is tame.

This is only
because you don't feed him

except for scraps—
meat torn like paper,
the occasional
lick of honey from
your hand.

He found you in the forest when he was young:

grinned, rolled
over to bare
his soft belly,
broken-cup teeth,
tongue
unfurling
like something
obscene.

He grew up

weaving
a quick ribbon of fur
between your ankles
almost
like sometimes
he was trying
to bring you
down to the floor.

The wolf wants to play games:

catch
fetch
lie down
play dead

He would like
to devour you, which is a way
of loving someone forever. This is why

you can't let him
into your bed.

Keep him weak.

He will curl
at your feet and growl
if you try
to kick
him away from the door.

Outside the wind
has sharp teeth, whines

Let the wolf keep you warm.

Dioscuri

We start with a map;
behind it is the actual world. Sometimes

our mind scrapes against it and the delicately illustrated rind
peels back: ornamental serpents bisected, borders scissor-cut

into absence, small towns and mountain ranges left with only
half a name—Look! behind these gaps

lurk balconies whose yellow windows are a door
we can't ever walk through, the bright glow

of McDonald's, a lord's mansion or Parliament,
a street of crowds where the couples walk by, two by two.

We are not of them. We are ourselves:
Janus-faced, twins in one body. My mind that says *yes,*

every little ship in the distance
unseen. My mind that says, *no, stay here.*

This cross-hatching is painful. What we see of the world
is freedom that looks like a barrier—

isn't a map supposed to lead somewhere?
We were given the wrong legend

my brother tells me, no proper way
to read the symbols.

My brother, myself;
my shadow, my other side.

I cover our head with our hood.
In one interpretation, we are split, disassociated;

from another angle, we are a body conjoined.

39

Parable

God sits in an ice-shack. Underneath
the frozen ocean, fish
swarm like little jeweled bees. God's tail
—swish, swish—brushes snow
from the door. Someone could enter

and sit down
somewhere where God is not
in the details but is fur,
and fish-hook fangs, staring
with his gleaming eyes. As for me,

I talk too much
and don't travel; sleep, wake,
and pile the produce on my plate
so eggplants glow like dark livers
and cherry tomatoes

are a stack of eyes. "I'm hungry,"
I say to God,
and hope he will devour me.
He curls his body like a comma, a furry river,
his back to me, and falls asleep.

Any questions will—if spoken—
freeze in frigid air, drop
like glass beads: clatter, shatter, roll away.
The door swings open, shut.
I go outside under constellations

and fill in the blank
space between the stars with favorite stories.
To change your life
you have to want to change your life: simple, simple.
There is another shack miles away.

Inside, the fox-red fire
leaps and flickers, casting shadows
on the drifts outside.
In those shadows, other stories. Time
to go inside.

You Keep On Working And I Will Continue Thinking About Wolves

If wolves run towards you
would the pack be a mat knife slicing snow if the forest
grew on a drafting table? You are architect

above it, sketching, saying, "there's
no future like the past." Outside, the sky
is very cold and also the gray sidewalk where people

are constellated. All day the streets fill up and empty. It seems
for a long time I had forgotten
my own skin and the workings of external

and internal organs. Thank you, hands,
bronchial branches, quick
fish of the tongue. This morning the dog

woke us with a whirring
noise in her throat like a tiny motor
or as if she'd become a small wind up bird

in her sleep. Body, you make everything so much less
alien and so much more so. The early pansies in the window box
opening up their little mouths.

Fresh Hells

1. *Limbo*
Hello, Facebook.

Hello, Facebook Silence.

2. *Lust*
You do not want to go on a second date with that lawyer, just admit it;
you only wonder if it's possible to be fucked out of your loneliness.

3. *Gluttony*
Is there kale?
There is no kale; all the bins are empty.
You know who else doesn't have kale?
All those people dying.
What's wrong with you that you aren't grateful?
Your cupboards are a cornucopia of all you have that you don't want.

4. *Greed*
Sandals with gold straps of a finer plastic, blue necklace, black dress.

For your book to finally be published on some minor but still notable press.

To love someone who loves you back.

Kids, maybe, even if your fertility might be an hourglass as the sand runs out.

An apartment where the faucets do not leak.

5. *Anger*
The nail salon radio station plays an extended version of "You've Got
a Friend" the week after one of your favorite friendships ends. The
rage that comes from being trapped with terrible music. How much
more than stifling the slide towards crying you want to type out "James
Taylor can go to hell," but one hand is in the bowl of water, the other
stilled motionless as Lucy paints meticulous red upon your nails. This is

probably for the better—you'd have wanted to send the text to the one who isn't speaking to you now anyway.

6. *Heresy*

"The soul dies when the body dies"—so say the Epicureans

It took so long to love the body; hating spiders, having spider veins.

Sometimes the body outlives the soul as any late night bar might show you.

I want to believe that something will outlast us, but I'm so often wrong.

There is an actual website called godhelpmeplease.com

7. *Violence*

Dante counts violence against the self: profligates, suicides.

A pack of cigarettes at the bodega costs $14.50.

The night of drinking will run another $95.

8. *Fraud*

Fraud involves intentional deception: a willfully false representation that harms the other for personal gain. In this it is different

from mistakes or false cognates/friends; for example, "fast" means "speedy" or, in German, "almost"; as in, we were swift and almost friends.

9. *Treachery*

Those who betray fidelity, confidence or trust
are found star-fished and limbs pinwheeling
beneath the frozen lake; eyes open, they can stare,

but cannot speak. So saith Dante,

who with his Virgil, climbed down Satan's ragged fur
to escape. There are so many different paths

to what either person could call betrayal. I would trade
being right for an ice-ax or a bonfire
to loosen the clogged rivers of our throats.

If My Life Were A Radio, Lately I Would Prefer Another Station

When I saw you lean against her at the bar, my mind
became a sad bodega: terrible stale pastries sheathed in cellophane

and, above, a harsh fluorescence. It's a shame
because in the fields behind my rib cage, horses made from lightning

kick and run. I would have liked to take you
on a road trip where the windshield clouds with snow

and we'd imagine that we drove through static.
Now, there is an entire country full of roadside motels

where we'll never sleep together! Not to mention wine cellars
and apple orchards. So be it. How often people orbit

to be half of someone else's binary star. A window box I walk past
on East 10th Street holds a row of tiny planets

buttoned into dirt: I mean purple cabbages there.
Occasionally I wish I could painlessly trepan the world

and bore a hole down to the brain of things. I'd like to see
the pulse amid gray matter

which is not to be confused with going to some mountaintop
to watch pulsars. Still, give me the right telescope and I would

since, the other night, I kept sketching asteroids in black ink on bar napkins,
little orbs unmoored in interstellar space. Last year's student

sends me a picture of snow. When I write back, my postcard
will be of crustaceans. All day long

my neighbor's children have been jumping off the stoop
like little frogs and singing. All day long I have been hungry

for crabs harvested from the sea. When they tell me in yoga be a bow,
I hear boat. I only want to be a weapon sometimes.

I think what I need are only proper tools and enough time
to rewire all the world's secret circuit boards.

Despite The Numerous Things I Might Fixate On, I Am Still Very Lucky To Go To Parties In Brooklyn And Share Cabs With Friends Coming Home

Wineglass a clear globe with the top sliced off;
in the bottom-half a red tidal pool where the sea urchins swirl
when my hand (immense pretend God) changes direction.

On the balcony, rain brushes
against gingko leaves. The whole sky
is an eyelid that's blinking. Inside are well-furnished rooms. It's nice

to smoke other people's cigarettes and learn about Nietzsche
who loved horses and believed having five hundred hands
was a necessary component of genius. I only have two

and a mind that is kitten-furred and distractible. Where
does one go with such knowledge? What do my hands
actually do? Brush my hair, sew on an occasional

button. In medieval times, despite numerous tasks
of survival and praying, monks all over Europe
made beautiful wall hangings from their brothers' dry bones.

Consider that entire process—not just assembly
but also the dusting. In all these years,
I have not saved even one fingernail paring or a shred

of the moon. True, I want to amass all the coins
that are love or the right words or actual money.
Sailing ships launch

from all ports and sink into the ocean.
In the mulch below salt water and at the end of the evening—
all these scattered gold doubloons.

Wild Rabbits Have Sharp Eyes

Which is another way of saying, everything you want to hide
blares like a motel's Vacant sign. How long it took

for you to tumble into sleeping on the couch, the bed stripped
except for piles of laundry you could not bring yourself

to put away. Do you remember when you didn't
live inside this city's constant siren, when you were

the teenager in the woods, wearing dark like a blanket, the night
studded with stars as many as your friends. It's just the past now:

the teenagers you later taught are all adults now.
They have children, lovers. You have a certain archive of a mind

that files away the beautiful impractical. For example: The Amish
cultivate saffron. For example: Octopi have three hearts and die

of starvation—the mothers stop eating to guard
their unhatched eggs. So you know things.

Knowledge doesn't fix the faucet whose drip stains
the white sink chlorine blue. Information is only your own hands

stroking your hips as you turn each night. What you would give
to be a wheat field during a storm. Stalks bending, seeded

by violent rain, and the sky a clotted
purple arch above you, lightening strikes that jolt you so you remember

no matter how dead you feel you are not dead.

Taking Stock Of Things

Where are my friends? On a road
trip to find monsters. I
am home alone, trying to fix

my life. This means coffee.
This means the Internet. What
are monsters? Trembling, disfigured,

and probably very lonely as they huddle
cold in their dark caves. Good morning, monster,
I see you've practiced

grinning through your boring
daily pain. Let's polish the gleaming surfaces
of these vulpine teeth. Last night

was someone's arms
crossed across his chest, making a door
that's latched. Here is another: field

of anxiety like being encircled
by swarming bees. Who would come near?
A third thing that prevents

calm breathing is lying down to sleep
where the bed's a pit in which I'm buried—
rapid shovelfuls of escalating numbers, debt

as dirt that clogs my nostrils, mouth and throat; weighs
the eyelids shut. What are solutions? An equation
worked out in pencil on graph paper; the process

by which a substance is dispersed; or a liquid
in which the medicine's dissolved. No math, no chemistry,
no medicine, but instead, lately, so many mornings

where daylight seeps in sickly
from night's shattered bottle and I go to bed
like a soldier, worn out from waging

this long campaign where finally I've infiltrated
opposition's lines to discover,
sleeping in their tents, myself as enemy.

Basic Zoology

Soon I will stop wanting things.
According to the Buddhists,
this is good—not quite nirvana
but on the path, almost
a place to nap, close
to a patch of clover.
For most other major world religions also,
this is right, although
I should still want God.
I am not sure what the Zoroastrians say
because my Internet access is down
and, religiously speaking, I was raised
in a forest by wolves. Wolves

do not want anything; they only need,
which is different. They require teeth
to sunder skin from flesh and gnaw
on sharp sticks of bone.
They need the long flutes
of their throats that lead
to their gullets; also pink tongues
to lap rainwater from ditches.
Being concerned neither
with the lustrousness of their fur
nor the smallness of their souls, they mate
only to propagate the species.
On some nights, they sing

under the white hole
of the moon, behind which
is God's terrible blankness.

So Late To The Party

that everyone left before you arrived. Only a few
stragglers to share champagne dregs

with you: sweet little shards
collecting in the back of your throat, swarming

like insects in a hive. Now, there goes
that thing you shouldn't

have said, buzzing
like a fat summer bee. All these

inappropriate comments and every other life
you could have led: sad astronaut,

dictator, mother—oh, go ahead, and try to lasso
anyone around to tell them your theories

of The Impossible Future Made Manifest, Ghost Voices
You Hear Under Water, or How Frequently

The Past Flies Back To Us
Like Migrating Birds. It's no wonder

you'll wander home feral
at the end of the night; cake crumbs honeying

your lip corners.

Catechism

In the morning, I look for the beloved
and the beloved is not there. In the bodega

I look and he is also not there,
peering intently into the refrigeration unit, checking expiration dates
for various fruited yoghurts and soft cheese.

The beloved is God.
The face in the mirror is mine. I have these high cheekbones

which are the last trace of Mongols racing their swift horses
across grassy plains.

I have these burst-blood-vessel constellated eyes.

The beloved who is God
is somewhere high up in the heavens.
He is not stretched out
drinking beer from a glass bottle as green as an astro-turfed lawn.

The lawn is unmown. Where is the beloved?
If I lie down in the wilderness to hear his voice like water
as it rushes through trees

there is an emptiness behind the sound
which is like opening the door
to a room full of one empty chair

even though I'd imagined one of my grandmothers
—miraculous, revived from the grave—
rocking back and forth, knitting new socks for my birthday.

The problem is that I believe in the beloved.
The beloved who is God
answering the telegrams of my prayers.
The beloved who is someone else's body.

The beloved who is me
and often does not even care so very much

for all the other beloveds. I wake up

and put my hands to this morning's task
of whatever needs to be done.

I Will Begin Tagging "Sad Robot Inc." On Numerous Surfaces Because I Am Sorry I Am Not Always Good At Certain Emotional Intimacies Shared Between Friends

The ficus drapes its one long vine around
the antique bottle placed beside it
on the windowsill. If today

I were not bitter,
I would find this sweet. Which is to say
that this evening I am not lying

about an impossible affection
between glass and plant. Last night Andy
told me he used to dream in high school

that he was a vampire
and would huddle at the attic window
to burn before he hurt anyone he loved. In return

I have no revelation, only analysis
of how the dream's an obvious stand-in
for whatever he might have feared within.

Of course it's better
that our secret selves are known. And yet
I would be flat

and shadow-thin and slip
out through the space
under each question's

quickly locking door. Scrutiny,
you terrify me. I am so entirely
tired of this world today

and how I disappoint it. I want all
my wishes granted or, lacking that,
to be in the low reaches of the ocean.

To be entirely contained
by layered scales
until I look like I am a short silver road

undulating past. Again it seems
I have asked for a shiny surface
to keep me safe beneath. I'm sorry. Listen,

if I knew how
to better skin myself
I would.

Later

The beloved becoming
a heap of cold sand.
This is the part where seabirds
sound like a murder. Where the waves
are nervous hands.

A Little Gothic Tale

Let's start with bells pealing in the steeple: sonorous brass
rolls back and forth, overturned metal boat

lashed with ropes in a mooring slip carved from dank air. The clapper
—little man in the center—bangs his head against walls. The bats scud away,

and Quasimodo pushes his adoptive father—ungainly comet—
to the stone floor where stained glass casts a broken kaleidoscope

across his shattered skull. This happens in a movie: black and white in 1923,
then with color thirty years later, and again in 1986. This happens

in a French book, in a translation, in a dream, in a flat animation
where the young lovers live, and the hunchback's rewarded

with a heartbreak he recovers from by the next frame as if it's so easy
to relinquish when you're ugly. This is a preferred monster:

pliable and afraid, grateful we don't avert our eyes from the horns,
wings, additional limbs, terrible skin, unpaid bills, unkempt hair, messy

apartment, everything one long scream of isolation. Frankenstein wants a mate
and so is chased away from the castle. The golem contents himself

with "truth" inscribed on his forehead and God's name under his tongue,
and it's enough, but only for a little while. Dracula needs blood,

but also to make more of his kind. No one wants to be lonely.
Even the fox-wife sheds her skin

so she stands naked and lovely in the garden. Take her hand.
She'll lead you to the warren under the fields,

the tunnels full of sharp teeth and soft fur, breathing
in a pile you can sleep in. The kits whine and clamber and bat at you

with their little paws. There's rabbit for dinner,
rank blood in your nose. Above ground, the reapers scythe hay

and their crescent-moon sickles glint in the sunlight
like torches or knives, and if they come any closer you might run away.

In The Museum Of What I've Been Thinking

This whole night was Cannot Sleep and so you watched
the bedroom window in the mirror and waited. Curtains

rose and fell. Imagined sailing, and for a minute the bed
was a boat to pilot, but the floor is stagnant water

and you ran aground. Outside, the streets are dark and darker.
When I say *you* I mean *I*, which is solipsism, but, whoever you are,

be awake. On a plane, sitting in the inverted funnel made
when light isolates the solitary reader

like an experiment in a long glass tube. On a train or bus stuck
in the same phenomenon. Or in your lover's kitchen

where you sip cold seltzer by the sink or in the back yard with the constellations
of metal cans you abandon open for stray cats. Before

the fish was skinned, its scales gleamed metallic too. As did the hook
that caught it and the river under stars and moon: silver, silver. Sometimes

my days feel layered with connections that shine
the same way certain routes light up

when you press a button on 3-D Children's Museum displays.
In the Revolutionary War room, we can follow

the path Paul Revere's horse took on that famous midnight ride.
Note the churches and their steeples

where the lanterns glowed and huge bells shaped like metal tulips
their alarums clanged. Down the corridor in Basic Biology, you'll find

the entire central nervous system branching out
and, next door, are veins and capillaries

like all the secret causeways ever dreamed of—static
as they unfold before you on the body's perfect illuminated map.

Cosmo Magazine Tells Me I'll Be Alone All My Life

How do you show vulnerability? Read
a book. Be somewhere at the border of private
and public space: on a bench at the park
where pigeons constellate around you.

Let the wrists turn their soft slope outwards
so the inner skin glows
faintly as white neon signs in the rain and your palms
flop open at your sides to show they are empty.

But I do this often and still stride
through the world as if no one would ever
dare touch me. To the turtle,
his shell. To me, the mantle of imperviousness

which is the sad last choice in all of the fairy tales.
Better seven league boots. Better the four winds
coiled in a sack, the Freudian goose
whose shit—excuse me, eggs—becomes money, or a cat

sporting boots and a buckler. Better almost anything
except the fates of the princesses which are to sleep,
to have one's hair pulled, to choke on an apple and sleep
in a glass coffin until some passing stranger

finds your cadaver beautiful. My god.
No wonder so many people I know are unhappy.
People love each other all over the world
and yet most of us are still dying. In mass graves.

In the tidy white beds of oncology wards.
In our own homes, aged, from terrible falls.
If my genetics hold true, I have at least another fifty years
ahead of me. I will order

magazine subscriptions in perpetuity and hoard
economy family-sized containers
of detergent and cereal. Immense paper towel
cylinders I can log roll through the years. If time is a river

let it carry me softly to the mall—
that grand clean temple of commerce
under whose lights everyone is so shiny.

Michigan 1986

Most days you wake to birds—first the loon's wail
like a sad mother behind the kitchen window, then the mourning dove
croons you into gray daybreak.

That was the year the auto industry died, which means factories emptied
the way toys are removed from a box by a child (red plastic dinosaur, spool of thread,
gnawed pencil stub, Barbie head, thimble).

Smoothing clear packing tape across the closed cardboard
is like running your finger across someone's shut lips, indicating *silence*.
I know this. I have seen it done.

If factories are shuttered, there is always a way in
for rain, stray cats, explorers. Window-glass stalactites. Walls are lichen—
soft, peeling. On the floor, oil

slicks shaded lakes. Shadows loom in the corners mastodon-huge.
What have you built? I've built nothing. But I have flown out over the lake
on a swing hung from an ash tree by my father. The rope

cuts into the bark, the tire is weighed down by children. Here,
a sharp zero against the sky. Go ahead,
add yourself in there.

String Theory

Imagine this: in a parallel
universe Tom gets up from the table for more coffee,

returns. So does my grandfather, from the trenches
without fearing thunder, and my other grandfather,

from the bottle and remembering
Russian soldiers' fists on his mother's door, that splintering.

Instead, no trenches, no soldiers. The gray childhood cat
doesn't slip through the cracked

open window to vanish forever out of frame. I take
my icons down from the shelf. I dust the pictures

and file them away. No one dies, ever. We all forget
to forget certain names: bodies we interred

in their little boxes; cities bombed to fragments, desolate
with weeds. The rubble rises up, every structure

rebuilds. No more necropolises. In the multiverse,
one door opens

and I sit with you, paring an apple into slices
thin as crescent moons,

a new night sky. If you take one, that means
you love me. In a different universe, three strangers

are playing cards. We're each someone else now.
In one universe, I am falling

asleep at this very second; in another I stare
at the ocean all day. In a third, we elope

but our friends are all dying. Somewhere else, I steal bread
to stop our daughter from crying,

but you're already gone. How does anyone
ever make this work? In one, you were conscripted

or died of consumption or I married for money
instead of for love. The multiverse is a door.

Any room, any door. I walk through
and keep opening

in this infinite trying to get it right.

I Do Not Want To Lose Anybody

The people I loved in kindergarten: arms and legs tender
as sticks of butter left out on the countertop
for hours on a blue ceramic plate.

In high school, a tangle of limbs
like branches from a downed tree and, in the background, the lake
full of scattered green leaves.

College also.

And after.

You do not call me anymore.

And yet I will stay up all night
drinking the distilled essence of potatoes. Luminescent as moons,
they glow under their skins in the dark earth.

I will eat olives: each one a world plucked from the brine.

In Like A Lion, Out Like A Lamb

Inside the ship that is my torso,
my lungs are dirty lanterns—Listen, downstairs,

the neighbor's laughter. It is a clatter
like gravel on a windshield. She slams doors.

This morning I've been opening windows. On the stoop,
the super's son catcalls passing girls. The tiny fig tree

stretches broad green hands towards the light.
Last night was a tavern

where all friends were walking shaky as the sea.
We called this a celebration,

and it was. Today, time is a train where every hour
is a compartment to sit in and read a book

while, outside, the landscape passes by.
This means the day is moving

all around me and I am going toward the night,
but also further: maybe to a lighthouse near the sea.

The beach will be gray and rocky. Tidal pools fill up
with seaweed tresses and translucent crabs whose claws

feel like feathers brushed across your palm.
Let's go. I am packing bags

and making sandwiches. It is time,
and I am almost ready to begin.

Notes

The New York Times is the source for the Cat Power review headline that appears in "Thank You Again, Brooklyn, for the Free Coffee."

"Sonnet" takes its first line from Richard Siken's "Dirty Valentine."

"Sublation" takes its title from a translation of the German word Aufheben, particularly as used by Hegel. The translated term, as I found it, holds three simultaneous and contradictory meanings: to raise/lift up, to put away/store for later use, and to negate.

The song referenced in "The Problem Is Not that God Does Not Exist So Much as that He Will Not Bargain with You" is "Snow" by the excellent band Girls in Trouble.

The line "I am all dead leaves" in "Guidance" owes a debt to Frank O'Hara's "Meditations in an Emergency."

"Dioscuri" came into being as part of Satellite Collective's *Telephone* project, an international multi-genre art experiment. The poem was written in response to a collage by Charlotte Smith of Sheffield, England. In Greek myth, the Dioscuri were the twins Castor and Pollux. Although their father was the highest of the Olympian gods, their mother was human and so only one of the twins was granted immortality. After Castor, the mortal twin, died, Pollux petitioned his father to let him share his immortality with his brother so the two spent alternate days on Mount Olympus as gods and in Hades as mortal shades.

"Fresh Hells" is both a reworking of Dante's 9 circles of Hell in the *Inferno*, but also a tip of the hat to Dorothy Parker's famous response "What fresh hell is this?" whenever her doorbell rang.

The title of "Wild Rabbits Have Sharp Eyes" is taken from Marjory Williams' classic children's story *The Velveteen Rabbit*.

David Lehman's comments about *So Late to the Party* first appeared in *Poet Lore's* "Poets Introducing Poets" feature.

ABOUT THE AUTHOR

Kate Angus's work has appeared in *The Atlantic, Tin House, The Awl, Verse Daily, Best New Poets 2010* and *Best New Poets 2014.* She is the recipient of the A Room of Her Own Foundation's "Orlando" prize and *The New York Times*'s "Teacher Who Made a Difference" award, as well as residencies from Interlochen Arts Academy, the Betsy Hotel's Writer's Room, Wildfjords Trail and the BAU Institute. Born and raised in Michigan, she currently lives in New York where she is the founding editor of Augury Books, the Creative Writing Advisory Board Member for The Mayapple Center for Arts and Humanities, and curates the Pen and Brush Presents reading series. More information can be found at www.kateangus.org.

Photo Credit: John David West

ABOUT THE PRESS

On 21 December 1817, the poet John Keats wrote his brothers, George and Thomas about the quality that forms a [wo]man of achievement, especially in literature." He said: "At one it struck me what quality went to form a man of achievement, especially in literature, and which Shakespeare possessed so enormously—I mean **negative capability**, that is when a man is capable of being in uncertainties, mysteries, doubts, without any irritable reaching after fact and reason."

This important statement about being capable of contemplating the world without the desire to try and reconcile contradictions and doubts became the philosophy behind the journal *Negative Capability*. The first issue was published in Mobile, Alabama in July 1981. At that time, the Advisory Editors were: David Diamond, Leon Driskell, Richard Eberhart, Dale Edmonds, Jay Higginbotham, Roald Hoffman, X.J. Kennedy, Richard Moore, Karl Shapiro, W.D. Snodgrass, Diane Wakoski, Eugene Walter and Sophie Wilkins. The journal became one of the more prominent journals in the United States. Negative Capability Press was started as well with the publication of *Louisiana Creole Poems*, translated by Calvin André Claudel and also published in 1981.

Negative Capability Press has been publishing quality books and a journal for 34 years. In the fall of 2014, a special anniversary issue was published entitled *Thirty-Three*. Publisher, Sue B. Walker, Ph.D. and Associate Publisher, Megan Cary, M.F.A. continue to be committed to publishing quality books of exciting and innovative poetry, fiction, and nonfiction. We work diligently with our authors and view our publishing endeavors as a mutual commitment toward excellence.

Negative Capability Press Catalog

Later, Knives & Trees	Maureen Alsop
So Late to the Party	Kate Angus
Pretty Marrow	Shanan Ballam
Hatchery of Tongues	Michael Bassett
Too Late to Kill Me So	Joe Berry
The Plumage of the Sun	Margaret Key Biggs
The Tongue of Angles	John Brugaletta
With My Head Rising Out of Water	John Brugaletta
Little Dragons	Michael Bugeja
Collage: A Tribute to Steven Owen Bailey	John Chambers
Taste of Wine and Gentian	John Chambers
Suite for Stefano and Luisa-Gatta	John Chambers
Louisiana Creole Poems	Calvin André Claudel
In love with the ghost	Kristina Marie Darling and Max Avi Kaplan
Middle Class American Proverb	John Davis
Autumn Legacy	Lloyd Dendinger
Sweet Aegis: Medusa Poems	Melissa Dickson

Literary Mobile: 10th Anniversary Edition	Rachel Fowler, ed.
The Sound of Falling	Vernon Fowlkes, Jr.
Jessie's Garden	Tony Fusco
An Uncharted Inch	Maurice Gandy
Measures to Movements	Diane Beth Garden
The World's A Small Town	Roger Granet
Drew: Poems from Blue Water	Robert Gray
I Wish that I Were Langston Hughes	Robert Gray
Jesus Walks the Southland	Robert Gray
Prophets of the Morning Light	Patricia Harkins-Pierre
A Day Like Today	Barbara Henning
Two Faint Lines in the Violet	Lissa Kiernan
Departures	Philip Kolin
What Came Before	Irene Latham
We Still Live Here	Celia Lewis
Dividing by Zero	Barry Marks
Sounding	Barry Marks
The World Keeps Turning to Light	Caryn Marriam-Goldberg

It's Best Not to Interrupt Her Experiments — Carlo Matos

Scotts Bluid by Exilet: Letters in Lallants Verse — Authur McLean

Three Visitors — Mark Mitchell

The Mouse Whole — Richard Moore

Equivocal Blessings — Mary Carol Moran

The Uniform House — Jim Murphy

Blama — Mary Elizabeth Murphy

Let Your Mind Run Free — Harry Myers

Barn Flight — Carolyn Page

Clutching Lambs — Janet Passehl

To Live and Write in Dixie — P.T. Paul

The Hero of the Revolution Serves Us Tea — Clela Reed

The Luftwaffe in Chaos — Nicholas Rinaldi

waitin' round the bend — Charles and Mary Rodning

The Girl in the Glass — Alexis Saunders

A Place Never Imagined — Alexis Saunders

Bearing the Print — Sue Scalf

Wake Up Laughing — Pat Schneider

Fair Haven	Vivian Shipley
Devil's Lane	Vivian Shipley
Perennial	Vivian Shipley
Traces of Presence	Betty Spence
And Finding No Mouse There	Vivian Smallwood
To Speak This Tongue	Louis Skipper
The Nights, The Days	Kathleen Thompson
Bodies	Alison Touster-Reed
Deeper than Monday Night Football	James Walker
Whatever Remembers Us	Sue Walker and John Chambers
Rueben's Mobile	Sue Walker and Kate Seawell
Life on the Line: Selections on Words & Healing	Sue Walker and Rosaly Roffman
Literary Mobile	Sue Walker with Mary M. Riser and John Hafner
Thirty-Three: An[niversary] Anthology	Sue Walker with Bailey Hammond, Karie Fugett and Rachel McMullen
Negative Capability, Vol. 34: The Body in D[ist]ress	Sue Brannan Walker with Megan Cary
Traveling My Shadow	Sue Brannan Walker

Seriously Meeting Karl Shapiro	Sue Brannan Walker
Ways of Knowing: Essays on Marge Piercy	Sue Brannan Walker and Gene Hamner
Sister Nun	Shanti Weiland
Learning to Tell Time	Joe Whitten